# My FOOD Diary

EATING DISORDER RECOVERY JOURNAL

**Date:** _06/06_

Mood: ☺ 😁 😎 😐 😤 ☹ 😠 😴   Hours Slept: **4hrs**

### How have you been feeling today?

Medium... I felt very stressed in the morning & didn't eat. The day got better.

### Track your food intake below:

*Morning:*

Black coffee.

*Afternoon:*

Tuna salad, bana

*Evening:*

Chilli and rice, few tortilla crisps. Grapes.

Any triggers experienced today? An unexpected bill this morning, which also triggered OCD behaviour.

## Extra Notes!

I really didn't want to eat, so I was proud that I overcame it. Avoiding suger and trying to fuel myself with healthy stuff!
Felt a craving in the late evening to binge but I ate some grapes instead and the urge did pass after a while.

| Thoughts | Time | Feelings |
|---|---|---|
| OCD counting behaviour came back and I did skip breakfast. My clothes felt really tight, but I knew it was in my head. | 9am | Stress! New bill! |
| Urge to skip on lunch but I resisted! | 1pm | Did not want food! |
| Really wanted sugar! Went for some grapes. The urge passed. | 10pm | Binge urge! |
| Goal tomorrow: *Aim for a good breakfast! | | |

# Notes

# Notes

# Notes

# Notes

# Date:_____

Mood:  ☺ 😃 😎 😐 😣 ☹ 😠 😤     Hours Slept:

## How have you been feeling today?

_____
_____
_____

## Track your food intake below:

Morning:

Afternoon:

Evening:

Any triggers experienced today? _____
_____

# Extra Notes!

_____
_____
_____
_____
_____
_____
_____

# Thoughts

| Time | Feelings |
|---|---|
| | |
| | |
| | |
| | |
| | |
| | |
| | |
| | |
| | |
| | |
| | |
| | |
| | |
| | |
| | |
| | |
| | |
| | |
| | |

Date:_____

Mood:  ☺ 😄 😇 😐 😒 🙁 😠 😵    Hours Slept:

## How have you been feeling today?

_____

_____

_____

## Track your food intake below:

*Morning:*

*Afternoon:*

*Evening:*

Any triggers experienced today? _____

_____

# Extra Notes!

_____

_____

_____

_____

_____

_____

# Thoughts

# Time

# Feelings

Date:_____

Mood:  ☺ 😄 😎 😐 😥 🙁 😣 😓     Hours Slept:

How have you been feeling today?

_____

_____

_____

Track your food intake below:

Morning:

Afternoon:

Evening:

Any triggers experienced today? _____

_____

Extra Notes!

_____

_____

_____

_____

_____

_____

## Thoughts

## Time

## Feelings

Date:_____

Mood:  ☺ 😃 😇 😐 😫 🙁 😠 😓     Hours Slept:

## How have you been feeling today?

_____
_____
_____

## Track your food intake below:

Morning:

Afternoon:

Evening:

Any triggers experienced today?

_____

# Extra Notes!

_____
_____
_____
_____
_____
_____
_____

# Thoughts

# Time

# Feelings

# Date: _____

Mood: ☺ 😃 😎 😐 😫 ☹ 😡 😤    Hours Slept: 

## How have you been feeling today?

_____

_____

_____

## Track your food intake below:

*Morning:*

*Afternoon:*

*Evening:*

Any triggers experienced today? _____

_____

# Extra Notes!

_____

_____

_____

_____

_____

_____

_____

# Thoughts

# Time

# Feelings

**Date:** _____

Mood: 😊 😄 😇 😐 😣 😟 😠 😎    Hours Slept: _____

## How have you been feeling today?

_____
_____
_____

## Track your food intake below:

*Morning:*

*Afternoon:*

*Evening:*

Any triggers experienced today? _____
_____

# Extra Notes!

_____
_____
_____
_____
_____
_____
_____
_____

# Thoughts

## Time

## Feelings

# Date: _____

Mood: ☺ 😄 😇 😐 😫 ☹ 😠 😓    Hours Slept:

## How have you been feeling today?

_____
_____
_____

## Track your food intake below:

**Morning:**

**Afternoon:**

**Evening:**

Any triggers experienced today? _____
_____

# Extra Notes!

_____
_____
_____
_____
_____
_____
_____

# Thoughts

# Time

# Feelings

| | |
|---|---|
| | |
| | |
| | |
| | |
| | |
| | |
| | |
| | |
| | |
| | |
| | |
| | |
| | |
| | |
| | |
| | |
| | |

# Date: _____

Mood: 😊 😄 😇 😐 🥴 🙁 😠 😎    Hours Slept: _____

## How have you been feeling today?

_____
_____
_____

## Track your food intake below:

*Morning:*

*Afternoon:*

*Evening:*

Any triggers experienced today? _____
_____

## Extra Notes!

_____
_____
_____
_____
_____
_____
_____

# Thoughts                    Time        Feelings

Date: _____

Mood:  ☺ 😄 😇 😐 😣 ☹ 😠 😓    Hours Slept: _____

## How have you been feeling today?

_____

_____

_____

## Track your food intake below:

Morning:

Afternoon:

Evening:

Any triggers experienced today? _____

_____

# Extra Notes!

_____

_____

_____

_____

_____

_____

_____

# Thoughts

# Time

# Feelings

**Date:** _____

Mood:  ☺ 😄 😇 😐 😣 🙁 😠 😎   Hours Slept: _____

## How have you been feeling today?

_____
_____
_____

## Track your food intake below:

**Morning:**

**Afternoon:**

**Evening:**

Any triggers experienced today? _____

_____

# Extra Notes!

_____
_____
_____
_____
_____
_____
_____

# Thoughts     Time     Feelings

Date:_____

Mood:  ☺ 😄 😇 😐 😫 🙁 😠 😵‍💫     Hours Slept:

## How have you been feeling today?

_____
_____
_____

## Track your food intake below:

*Morning:*

*Afternoon:*

*Evening:*

Any triggers experienced today? _____
_____

# Extra Notes!

_____
_____
_____
_____
_____
_____
_____

# Thoughts

# Time

# Feelings

# Date: _____

Mood:  ☺ 😄 😇 😐 😷 ☹ 😠 😓     Hours Slept: _____

## How have you been feeling today?

_____
_____
_____

## Track your food intake below:

**Morning:**

**Afternoon:**

**Evening:**

Any triggers experienced today? _____

_____

# Extra Notes!

_____
_____
_____
_____
_____
_____
_____
_____

# Thoughts

# Time

# Feelings

Date: _____

Mood: ☺ 😃 😇 😐 😣 ☹ 😠 😓    Hours Slept: _____

How have you been feeling today?
_____
_____
_____

Track your food intake below:

Morning:

Afternoon:

Evening:

Any triggers experienced today? _____
_____

# Extra Notes!

_____
_____
_____
_____
_____
_____
_____
_____

# Thoughts

| Time | Feelings |
|------|----------|
|      |          |
|      |          |
|      |          |
|      |          |
|      |          |
|      |          |
|      |          |
|      |          |
|      |          |
|      |          |
|      |          |
|      |          |
|      |          |
|      |          |
|      |          |
|      |          |
|      |          |
|      |          |

Date: _____

Mood:  ☺ 😄 😇 😐 😫 🙁 😠 😎    Hours Slept: _____

## How have you been feeling today?

_____

_____

_____

## Track your food intake below:

*Morning:*

*Afternoon:*

*Evening:*

Any triggers experienced today? _____

_____

# Extra Notes!

_____

_____

_____

_____

_____

_____

# Thoughts            Time            Feelings

# Date: _____

Mood: 😊 😃 😇 😐 😣 🙁 😠 😵‍💫   Hours Slept: 

## How have you been feeling today?

_____
_____
_____

## Track your food intake below:

Morning:
_____

Afternoon:
_____

Evening:
_____

Any triggers experienced today? _____
_____

## Extra Notes!

_____
_____
_____
_____
_____
_____
_____

# Thoughts

| Time | Feelings |
|------|----------|
|      |          |
|      |          |
|      |          |
|      |          |
|      |          |
|      |          |
|      |          |
|      |          |
|      |          |
|      |          |
|      |          |
|      |          |
|      |          |
|      |          |
|      |          |
|      |          |
|      |          |
|      |          |
|      |          |

**Date:** _____

Mood:  😊 😄 😇 😐 😫 🙁 😠 😎    Hours Slept: _____

### How have you been feeling today?

_____
_____
_____

### Track your food intake below:

**Morning:**

**Afternoon:**

**Evening:**

Any triggers experienced today? _____
_____

# Extra Notes!

_____
_____
_____
_____
_____
_____
_____

# Thoughts

# Time

# Feelings

# Date: _____

Mood: 😊 😄 😇 😐 😫 🙁 😠 😒   Hours Slept: _____

## How have you been feeling today?

_____

_____

_____

## Track your food intake below:

*Morning:*

*Afternoon:*

*Evening:*

Any triggers experienced today? _____

_____

# Extra Notes!

_____

_____

_____

_____

_____

_____

_____

# Thoughts

| Time | Feelings |
|------|----------|
|      |          |
|      |          |
|      |          |
|      |          |
|      |          |
|      |          |
|      |          |
|      |          |
|      |          |
|      |          |
|      |          |
|      |          |
|      |          |
|      |          |
|      |          |
|      |          |
|      |          |
|      |          |

Date: _____

Mood: 😊 😄 😇 😑 😫 🙁 😠 😈    Hours Slept: _____

## How have you been feeling today?

_____
_____
_____

## Track your food intake below:

Morning:

Afternoon:

Evening:

Any triggers experienced today?

_____
_____

## Extra Notes!

_____
_____
_____
_____
_____
_____

# Thoughts     Time     Feelings

# Date:_____

Mood:  😊 😄 😇 😐 😣 🙁 😠 😴     Hours Slept:

## How have you been feeling today?

_____
_____
_____

## Track your food intake below:

*Morning:*

*Afternoon:*

*Evening:*

Any triggers experienced today?
_____

# Extra Notes!

_____
_____
_____
_____
_____
_____
_____

# Thoughts

| Time | Feelings |
|------|----------|
|      |          |
|      |          |
|      |          |
|      |          |
|      |          |
|      |          |
|      |          |
|      |          |
|      |          |
|      |          |
|      |          |
|      |          |
|      |          |
|      |          |
|      |          |
|      |          |
|      |          |
|      |          |

Date:_____

Mood:  😊 😄 😇 😑 😥 ☹️ 😠 😎    Hours Slept:

## How have you been feeling today?

_____
_____

_____

## Track your food intake below:

Morning:

Afternoon:

Evening:

Any triggers experienced today?

_____

_____

# Extra Notes!

_____
_____
_____
_____
_____
_____
_____

# Thoughts

# Time

# Feelings

Date: _____

Mood:  ☺ 😄 😇 😐 😣 ☹ 😠 😎    Hours Slept: _____

## How have you been feeling today?

_____

_____

_____

## Track your food intake below:

Morning:

Afternoon:

Evening:

Any triggers experienced today?

_____

# Extra Notes!

_____

_____

_____

_____

_____

_____

_____

# Thoughts

# Time

# Feelings

# Date: _____

Mood: 😊 😄 😎 😐 😫 🙁 😠 😵‍💫    Hours Slept: _____

## How have you been feeling today?

_____

_____

_____

## Track your food intake below:

**Morning:**

**Afternoon:**

**Evening:**

Any triggers experienced today? _____

_____

# Extra Notes!

_____

_____

_____

_____

_____

_____

# Thoughts

# Time

# Feelings

Date:_____

Mood:  ☺ 😄 😇 😐 😫 🙁 😡 😒    Hours Slept:

## How have you been feeling today?

_____

_____

_____

## Track your food intake below:

*Morning:*

*Afternoon:*

*Evening:*

Any triggers experienced today?

_____

# Extra Notes!

_____

_____

_____

_____

_____

_____

_____

# Thoughts

# Time

# Feelings

**Date:** _____

Mood: 😊 😄 😇 😐 😩 ☹️ 😠 😎    Hours Slept: _____

## How have you been feeling today?

_____

_____

_____

## Track your food intake below:

*Morning:*

_____

*Afternoon:*

_____

*Evening:*

_____

Any triggers experienced today? _____

_____

## Extra Notes!

_____

_____

_____

_____

_____

_____

# Thoughts

| Time | Feelings |
|------|----------|
|      |          |
|      |          |
|      |          |
|      |          |
|      |          |
|      |          |
|      |          |
|      |          |
|      |          |
|      |          |
|      |          |
|      |          |
|      |          |
|      |          |
|      |          |
|      |          |
|      |          |
|      |          |
|      |          |

Date:_____

Mood:  ☺ 😄 😇 😐 😣 🙁 😠 😔    Hours Slept:

## How have you been feeling today?

_____
_____
_____

## Track your food intake below:

Morning:

Afternoon:

Evening:

Any triggers experienced today?

_____

# Extra Notes!

_____
_____
_____
_____
_____
_____
_____

# Thoughts

# Time

# Feelings

# Date: _____

Mood:  ☺ 😄 😇 😐 🥵 🙁 😠 🥴    Hours Slept: _____

## How have you been feeling today?

_____
_____
_____

## Track your food intake below:

*Morning:*



*Afternoon:*



*Evening:*



Any triggers experienced today?
_____
_____

# Extra Notes!

_____
_____
_____
_____
_____
_____

# Thoughts

| Time | Feelings |
|------|----------|
|      |          |
|      |          |
|      |          |
|      |          |
|      |          |
|      |          |
|      |          |
|      |          |
|      |          |
|      |          |
|      |          |
|      |          |
|      |          |
|      |          |
|      |          |
|      |          |
|      |          |
|      |          |
|      |          |

Date: _____

Mood:  😊 😄 😇 😐 😣 🙁 😡 😎     Hours Slept:

## How have you been feeling today?

_____
_____
_____

## Track your food intake below:

Morning:

Afternoon:

Evening:

Any triggers experienced today?

_____

## Extra Notes!

_____
_____
_____
_____
_____
_____
_____

# Thoughts

# Time

# Feelings

|  |  |
|---|---|
|  |  |
|  |  |
|  |  |
|  |  |
|  |  |
|  |  |
|  |  |
|  |  |
|  |  |
|  |  |
|  |  |
|  |  |
|  |  |
|  |  |
|  |  |
|  |  |
|  |  |
|  |  |

**Date:** _____

Mood: 😊 😃 😇 😐 😣 🙁 😠 😪    Hours Slept: _____

## How have you been feeling today?

_____

_____

_____

## Track your food intake below:

**Morning:**

**Afternoon:**

**Evening:**

Any triggers experienced today? _____

_____

## Extra Notes!

_____

_____

_____

_____

_____

_____

# Thoughts

| Time | | Feelings |
|---|---|---|
| | | |
| | | |
| | | |
| | | |
| | | |
| | | |
| | | |
| | | |
| | | |
| | | |
| | | |
| | | |
| | | |
| | | |
| | | |
| | | |
| | | |
| | | |

Date:_____

Mood:  ☺ 😄 😇 😐 😣 🙁 😠 😓    Hours Slept:

## How have you been feeling today?

_____
_____
_____

## Track your food intake below:

*Morning:*
_____

*Afternoon:*
_____

*Evening:*
_____

Any triggers experienced today?
_____

## Extra Notes!

_____
_____
_____
_____
_____
_____
_____

# Thoughts

| | Time | Feelings |
|---|---|---|
| | | |
| | | |
| | | |
| | | |
| | | |
| | | |
| | | |
| | | |
| | | |
| | | |
| | | |
| | | |
| | | |
| | | |
| | | |
| | | |
| | | |
| | | |

**Date:** _____

Mood: 😊 😃 😇 😐 😫 🙁 😠 🥴    Hours Slept: 

## How have you been feeling today?

_____
_____
_____

## Track your food intake below:

**Morning:**

**Afternoon:**

**Evening:**

Any triggers experienced today? _____
_____

# Extra Notes!

_____
_____
_____
_____
_____
_____

# Thoughts

| | Time | Feelings |
|---|---|---|
| | | |
| | | |
| | | |
| | | |
| | | |
| | | |
| | | |
| | | |
| | | |
| | | |
| | | |
| | | |
| | | |
| | | |
| | | |
| | | |
| | | |
| | | |

Date:_____

Mood:  ☺ ☺ 😇 😐 😣 🙁 😠 😤    Hours Slept:

## How have you been feeling today?

_____

_____

_____

## Track your food intake below:

Morning:

Afternoon:

Evening:

Any triggers experienced today?

_____

## Extra Notes!

_____

_____

_____

_____

_____

_____

# Thoughts

| | Time | Feelings |
|---|---|---|
| | | |
| | | |
| | | |
| | | |
| | | |
| | | |
| | | |
| | | |
| | | |
| | | |
| | | |
| | | |
| | | |
| | | |
| | | |
| | | |
| | | |
| | | |

**Date:** _____

Mood: 😊 😄 😇 😑 😫 😟 😠 😴   Hours Slept: _____

## How have you been feeling today?

_____

_____

_____

## Track your food intake below:

*Morning:*

*Afternoon:*

*Evening:*

Any triggers experienced today?

_____

# Extra Notes!

_____

_____

_____

_____

_____

# Thoughts

| | Time | Feelings |
|---|---|---|
| | | |
| | | |
| | | |
| | | |
| | | |
| | | |
| | | |
| | | |
| | | |
| | | |
| | | |
| | | |
| | | |
| | | |
| | | |
| | | |
| | | |
| | | |
| | | |

# Date: _____

Mood: 😊 😄 😇 😐 😣 ☹️ 😠 😵‍💫   Hours Slept: _____

## How have you been feeling today?

_____

_____

_____

## Track your food intake below:

*Morning:*

*Afternoon:*

*Evening:*

Any triggers experienced today?

_____

## Extra Notes!

_____

_____

_____

_____

_____

_____

# Thoughts

# Time

# Feelings

# Date: _____

Mood: 😊 😃 😇 😑 😣 🙁 😠 😵‍💫   Hours Slept: _____

## How have you been feeling today?

_____

_____

_____

## Track your food intake below:

**Morning:**

**Afternoon:**

**Evening:**

Any triggers experienced today? _____

_____

# Extra Notes!

_____

_____

_____

_____

_____

_____

# Thoughts

# Time

# Feelings

Date:_____

Mood:  ☺ 😄 😇 😐 😫 🙁 😠 😣     Hours Slept:

## How have you been feeling today?

_____
_____
_____

## Track your food intake below:

*Morning:*

*Afternoon:*

*Evening:*

Any triggers experienced today?
_____
_____

# Extra Notes!

_____
_____
_____
_____
_____
_____
_____

# Thoughts

# Time

# Feelings

Date:_____

Mood:  😊 😄 😇 😐 😣 🙁 😠 😵   Hours Slept:

## How have you been feeling today?

_____
_____
_____

## Track your food intake below:

Morning:

Afternoon:

Evening:

Any triggers experienced today?
_____
_____

# Extra Notes!

_____
_____
_____
_____
_____
_____
_____

# Thoughts

# Time

# Feelings

## Date:_____

Mood:  ☺ ☺ 😇 😐 😫 ☹ 😠 😴    Hours Slept: _____

### How have you been feeling today?

_____
_____
_____

### Track your food intake below:

**Morning:**

**Afternoon:**

**Evening:**

Any triggers experienced today?

_____
_____

## Extra Notes!

_____
_____
_____
_____
_____
_____
_____

# Thoughts     Time     Feelings

**Date:** _____

Mood: ☺ 😄 😇 😐 😫 🙁 😠 🥴   Hours Slept: _____

## How have you been feeling today?

_____

_____

_____

## Track your food intake below:

*Morning:*

*Afternoon:*

*Evening:*

Any triggers experienced today?
_____

_____

# Extra Notes!

_____

_____

_____

_____

_____

_____

## Thoughts

| Time | Feelings |
|------|----------|
|      |          |
|      |          |
|      |          |
|      |          |
|      |          |
|      |          |
|      |          |
|      |          |
|      |          |
|      |          |
|      |          |
|      |          |
|      |          |
|      |          |
|      |          |
|      |          |
|      |          |
|      |          |
|      |          |

Date: _____

Mood: ☺ 😄 😇 😑 🤒 🙁 😠 🥴     Hours Slept:

## How have you been feeling today?

_____
_____
_____

## Track your food intake below:

*Morning:*

*Afternoon:*

*Evening:*

Any triggers experienced today?

_____

# Extra Notes!

_____
_____
_____
_____
_____
_____
_____

# Thoughts

| | Time | Feelings |
|---|---|---|
| | | |
| | | |
| | | |
| | | |
| | | |
| | | |
| | | |
| | | |
| | | |
| | | |
| | | |
| | | |
| | | |
| | | |
| | | |
| | | |
| | | |
| | | |
| | | |

**Date:** _____

Mood: 😊 😄 😇 😐 😫 🙁 😠 😵    Hours Slept: _____

### How have you been feeling today?

_____

_____

_____

### Track your food intake below:

*Morning:*

*Afternoon:*

*Evening:*

Any triggers experienced today?

_____

_____

# Extra Notes!

_____

_____

_____

_____

_____

# Thoughts

# Time

# Feelings

**Date:** _____

Mood:  😊 😄 😇 😐 😣 🙁 😠 😓   Hours Slept: _____

## How have you been feeling today?

_____

_____

_____

## Track your food intake below:

*Morning:*

_____

*Afternoon:*

_____

*Evening:*

_____

Any triggers experienced today?

_____

## Extra Notes!

_____

_____

_____

_____

_____

_____

# Thoughts

| Time | Feelings |
|---|---|
| | |
| | |
| | |
| | |
| | |
| | |
| | |
| | |
| | |
| | |
| | |
| | |
| | |
| | |
| | |
| | |
| | |
| | |
| | |

**Date:** _____

Mood: 😊 😃 😇 😐 😣 🙁 😠 😵   Hours Slept: _____

## How have you been feeling today?

_____
_____
_____

## Track your food intake below:

*Morning:*

*Afternoon:*

*Evening:*

Any triggers experienced today?

_____

# Extra Notes!

_____
_____
_____
_____
_____
_____

# Thoughts

| Time | Feelings |
|---|---|
| | |
| | |
| | |
| | |
| | |
| | |
| | |
| | |
| | |
| | |
| | |
| | |
| | |
| | |
| | |
| | |
| | |
| | |

# Date: _____

Mood: 😊 😄 😇 😐 😣 🙁 😡 😎    Hours Slept: _____

## How have you been feeling today?

_____

_____

_____

## Track your food intake below:

*Morning:*

_____

*Afternoon:*

_____

*Evening:*

_____

Any triggers experienced today?

_____

## Extra Notes!

_____

_____

_____

_____

_____

_____

# Thoughts

| Time | Feelings |
|---|---|
|  |  |
|  |  |
|  |  |
|  |  |
|  |  |
|  |  |
|  |  |
|  |  |
|  |  |
|  |  |
|  |  |
|  |  |
|  |  |
|  |  |
|  |  |
|  |  |
|  |  |
|  |  |
|  |  |

**Date:**_____

Mood:  ☺ 😀 😇 😐 😫 🙁 😠 😜   Hours Slept:

## How have you been feeling today?

_____
_____
_____

## Track your food intake below:

*Morning:*

*Afternoon:*

*Evening:*

Any triggers experienced today?
_____
_____

# Extra Notes!

_____
_____
_____
_____
_____
_____

# Thoughts

| | Time | Feelings |
|---|---|---|
| | | |
| | | |
| | | |
| | | |
| | | |
| | | |
| | | |
| | | |
| | | |
| | | |
| | | |
| | | |
| | | |
| | | |
| | | |
| | | |
| | | |
| | | |
| | | |

# Date: _____

Mood: 😊 😄 😇 😐 😣 🙁 😠 😓     Hours Slept: _____

## How have you been feeling today?

_____
_____
_____

## Track your food intake below:

**Morning:**

**Afternoon:**

**Evening:**

## Any triggers experienced today?

_____

# Extra Notes!

_____
_____
_____
_____
_____
_____
_____
_____

# Thoughts

# Time

# Feelings

# Date: _____

Mood:  ☺ 😄 😇 😐 😣 ☹ 😠 😤    Hours Slept: _____

## How have you been feeling today?

_____

_____

_____

## Track your food intake below:

**Morning:**

**Afternoon:**

**Evening:**

Any triggers experienced today?

_____

_____

# Extra Notes!

_____

_____

_____

_____

_____

_____

# Thoughts

| Time | Feelings |
|------|----------|
|      |          |
|      |          |
|      |          |
|      |          |
|      |          |
|      |          |
|      |          |
|      |          |
|      |          |
|      |          |
|      |          |
|      |          |
|      |          |
|      |          |
|      |          |
|      |          |
|      |          |
|      |          |
|      |          |

Date: _____

Mood:  ☺ 😄 😇 😐 😫 🙁 😠 😤     Hours Slept: _____

## How have you been feeling today?

_____

_____

_____

## Track your food intake below:

*Morning:*

*Afternoon:*

*Evening:*

Any triggers experienced today?

_____

# Extra Notes!

_____

_____

_____

_____

_____

_____

# Thoughts

| Time | Feelings |
|------|----------|
|      |          |
|      |          |
|      |          |
|      |          |
|      |          |
|      |          |
|      |          |
|      |          |
|      |          |
|      |          |
|      |          |
|      |          |
|      |          |
|      |          |
|      |          |
|      |          |
|      |          |
|      |          |
|      |          |

**Date:** _____

Mood:  ☺ 😄 😎 😐 😫 🙁 😠 😈    Hours Slept: _____

### How have you been feeling today?

_____

_____

_____

### Track your food intake below:

*Morning:*

*Afternoon:*

*Evening:*

Any triggers experienced today? _____

_____

# Extra Notes!

_____

_____

_____

_____

_____

_____

# Thoughts     Time     Feelings

# Date:_____

Mood:  ☺ 😄 😇 😐 😫 🙁 😠 😓    Hours Slept: 

## How have you been feeling today?

_____

_____

_____

## Track your food intake below:

*Morning:*

_____

*Afternoon:*

_____

*Evening:*

_____

Any triggers experienced today?

_____

# Extra Notes!

_____

_____

_____

_____

_____

_____

_____

# Thoughts

| Time | Feelings |
|---|---|
| | |
| | |
| | |
| | |
| | |
| | |
| | |
| | |
| | |
| | |
| | |
| | |
| | |
| | |
| | |
| | |
| | |
| | |
| | |

## Date: _____

Mood: 🙂 😄 😇 😐 😣 🙁 😠 😵‍💫　Hours Slept: _____

### How have you been feeling today?

_____
_____
_____

### Track your food intake below:

**Morning:**

**Afternoon:**

**Evening:**

Any triggers experienced today?

_____

# Extra Notes!

_____
_____
_____
_____
_____
_____

# Thoughts

| Time | Feelings |
|---|---|
| | |
| | |
| | |
| | |
| | |
| | |
| | |
| | |
| | |
| | |
| | |
| | |
| | |
| | |
| | |
| | |
| | |
| | |
| | |

Made in the USA
Las Vegas, NV
05 October 2023

78574551R00063